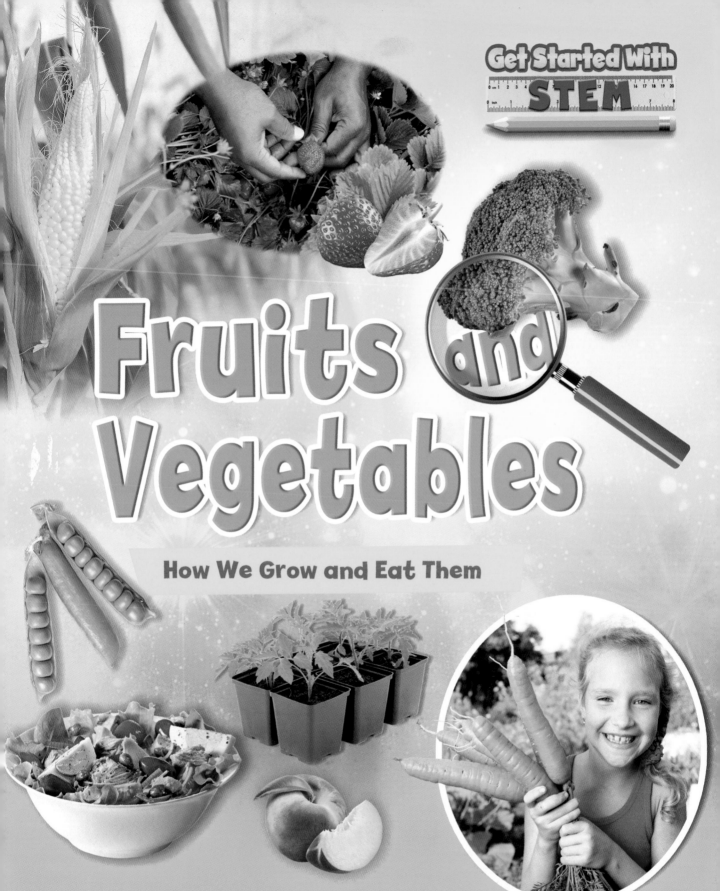

Get Started With STEM

Fruits and Vegetables

How We Grow and Eat Them

by Ruth Owen

Ruby Tuesday Books

Published in 2022 by Ruby Tuesday Books Ltd.

Editor: Mark J. Sachner
Designer: Emma Randall
Production: John Lingham

Photo credits:
Alamy: 10B (Media World Images); Shutterstock: Cover and 1 (pixelheadphoto/Gladskikh Tatiana), 2, 4 (zi3000/Kenishirotie/Stefan Malloch/Rawpixel.com), 5, 6–7, 8T, 8C (FotoDuets), 8B, 9T (yoshi0511), 10T (ntdanai), 11T (Bearfotos), 12T (Alan Morris), 12B, 13T (Filip Ilic Novi Sad), 13B, 14, 15T (UpScope), 15B, 16, 16BR (NokHoOkNoi), 17 (Gardens by Designs), 18T (tmcphotos), 18–19, 20T (Ilike), 20B, 21T (Seda Bodur), 21C (Marina Green), 21BL (Marina Green), 22 (kurbanov), 23T (Imfoto), 23B (vallefrias), 24T, 24C (hans engbers), 24B (barmalini), 25T (Trialist), 26, 27T (Radovan1), 27B (oksana2010), 28T (Stefanie Keller), 28C (Tualek Photo), 28B (Magdalena Kowalik), 29T (Elena Masiutkina), 30–31.

Library of Congress Control Number: 2021919972

Print (Hardback) ISBN 978-1-78856-274-4
Print (Paperback) ISBN 978-1-78856-275-1
eBook PDF 978-1-78856-276-8
ePub 978-1-78856-277-5
Published in Minneapolis, MN, USA
Printed in the United States

www.rubytuesdaybooks.com

Contents

Words shown in **bold** in the text are explained in the glossary.

The download button shows there are free worksheets or other resources available. Go to:

www.rubytuesdaybooks.com/getstarted

Growing Our Food

We eat fruits and vegetables in lots of different ways. But where do they come from?

Shoppers buy these foods from supermarkets, local shops, and markets.

A supermarket

A farmers' market

But before we can buy vegetables and fruits, farmers have to grow them.

How do you think these foods grow?

(The answers are at the bottom of the page.)

Under the ground?

Which ones grow on a tree?

Above ground?

Beets

Apples

Peas

Peaches

Cherries

Carrots

Cucumbers

Some people grow fruit and vegetables in their own gardens or a community garden.

Tomatoes

Broccoli

Oranges

Potatoes

Onions

What Is a Vegetable?

A vegetable is a part of a plant that people eat.

Carrot plant

Beet plant

Radish plant

Onion plant

Root

Root

Root

Bulb

We eat the fat **roots** of carrot, beet, and radish plants.

An onion plant grows from a **bulb**. The crunchy, tasty onion that we eat is actually the bulb.

Cabbages

We eat the leaves of lettuce and cabbage plants.

Lettuce leaves

Lettuce

Some of the vegetables people like to eat are **seeds**.

Beans and sweet corn are both types of seeds.

Haricot beans

Sweet corn

Haricot beans are used to make baked beans.

Let's Talk

What are the parts of a broccoli plant that we eat called?

How Does Broccoli Grow?

Buds

Stem

We eat the **stems** of broccoli plants.

We also eat the **buds** that will become the plant's flowers. But how does broccoli grow?

Broccoli seeds

On a farm, broccoli seeds are planted in trays of compost and placed in a warm greenhouse.

Seedling

The seeds grow into broccoli seedlings.

In spring, the seedlings are planted outside in a field.

Seedlings in tray

Planting machine

Broccoli seedling

A machine drops each little plant into the soil and presses it into place.

Now, rain and sunshine will help the plants to grow.

Broccoli belongs to the same plant family as cabbages, cauliflowers, and kale.

Red cabbage   Kale   Cauliflower

Let's Investigate Broccoli

Broccoli seedlings grow throughout the spring.

Crown

Leaf

By summer, the broccoli crowns are ready to be harvested.

Some broccoli plants are left to grow in the greenhouse. They produce flowers and then seeds. The seeds are used to grow next year's broccoli crop.

A team of workers follows a tractor across the field.

The workers use large, sharp knives to cut a broccoli crown from each plant.

Then the broccoli is put into boxes and is ready to be delivered to shops.

Be a Scientist!

What do broccoli flowers look like?

Gather your equipment:
- A broccoli crown
- A knife and cutting board
- 3 glasses or glass jars
- Water
- A notebook and pen
- A hand lens or magnifying glass

1. Very carefully cut three pieces of broccoli from the crown. Cut each piece so its stem is as long as possible.

2. Fill the glasses with water almost to the top.

3. Place a piece of broccoli into each glass.

What do you think will happen to the broccoli? How will it look? Write your predictions in your notebook.

4. Now check in on your experiment each day and observe what happens.

5. If you need to add more water to the glasses (or replace the water to freshen it), that's fine.

What do you observe happening to the broccoli? Use your hand lens or magnifying glass to take a close look.

6. Record your results in your notebook. Draw what happens or take a photo.

Growing Carrots

On a carrot farm, the fields are plowed and a machine removes any stones from the soil.

Stone remover

If a carrot grows around a stone, it can form an unusual shape!

Next, tiny carrot seeds are planted in the soil.

Carrot seeds

Carrot plants

About four months later, the carrots are fully grown.

A harvesting machine pulls them from the soil and cuts off the stalks and leaves.

Finally, a truck takes them to a factory, where they are washed and sorted by size.

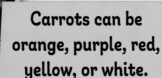

Muddy carrots

Carrots can be orange, purple, red, yellow, or white.

Let's Talk

What do you think pea plant seeds look like?

13

Frozen!

The fresh, frozen, or canned peas that we eat are actually a pea plant's seeds!

Dried peas for seeds

Pea flowers

Farmers plant pea seeds in rows in fields.

New pod

Tiny peas forming

Dying flowers

Pea plant

The plants grow, produce flowers, and then make pods that contain the peas, or new seeds.

Peas in a pod

A huge machine called a pea viner pulls the pea plants from the soil.

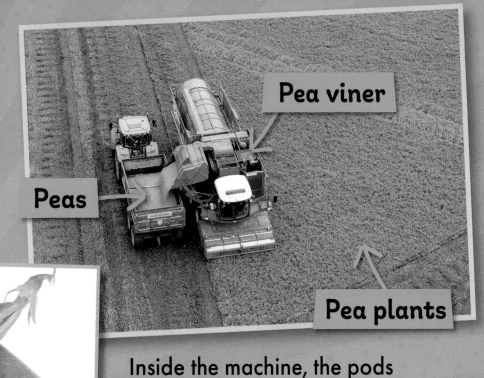

Pea viner

Peas

Pea plants

Inside the machine, the pods are gently spun around so they open, and the peas fall out.

At a factory, the peas are washed.

Then a machine called a flow freezer blows icy air onto the peas, which freezes them.

It takes just 2.5 hours to harvest, freeze, and pack peas in bags ready to go to shops! Farmers save and dry some peas to plant next year.

Frozen peas

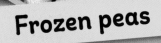

Growing Corn on the Cob

Sweet corn comes from maize (corn) plants. The tiny yellow parts we eat are seeds called kernels.

Kernels

Canned corn

To grow sweet corn, kernels are planted in soil.

Silks

Cob

Corn on the cob

Frozen corn

After 15 weeks, small cobs grow from each plant's stem.

Each cob has hairlike silks on its tip.

Flower

Plants

Ripe corn on the cob

A flower grows at the top of each plant's stem and releases **pollen**.

The pollen is blown onto the cobs' silks by the wind.

This **pollinates** the cobs. Then they grow bigger and fatter.

When the silks turn brown, the cobs are ready to be picked and eaten.

Be an Inventor

At factories, kernels are removed from corn cobs. Then the kernels can be frozen or put into cans.

What kind of machine could strip millions of kernels from cobs?

Gather your equipment:
• A corn on the cob
• Paper, pencils, or pens

1. Carefully observe the cob. (If you don't have a cob, you can look at a photo.)

Is it easy or difficult to remove the kernels from the cob with your fingers?

2. Now think about and sketch some ideas for your machine.

How will the cobs get into your machine? What kind of energy will power your machine?
What kind of tool could remove the kernels?

3. Draw a diagram of your machine. Label its parts and write a short description of how it does its job.

What is your machine called?

What Is a Fruit?

This question can be a little tricky to answer.

We might say it's a juicy, sweet part of a plant such as an apple or orange.

But in science, the answer is different.

A fruit is actually the part of a plant where its seeds grow.

Apple seeds

Orange seeds

Apples and oranges are fruits. But so are tomatoes, peppers, and squashes!

Squash seeds

Tomato seeds

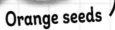

Green pepper seeds

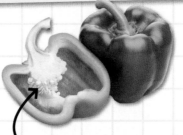

There are lots of fruits that we think of as vegetables. This is probably because we cook and eat them with other savory foods as part of our main meals.

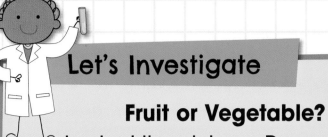

Let's Investigate

Fruit or Vegetable?

Look at the pictures. Do you think each food is a fruit or a vegetable?

Green beans

Pumpkin

Parsnips

Plums

Avocados

Blueberries

Leeks

Cucumber

Watermelon

Let's Talk

Is a pea pod a fruit or a vegetable?

(The answers for page 19 are on page 32.)

19

Growing Tomatoes

People grow and eat tomatoes all over the world.

Seeds

To grow tomatoes, a farmer or gardener plants tomato seeds in soil.

Flowers

Seedling

A seedling sprouts from each tiny seed and starts to grow.

Tomato plant

When a tomato plant is about 12 weeks old, it grows yellow flowers.

Bees and other insects pollinate the flowers.

Then the flowers die, and seeds start to grow inside tiny green fruits.

Bumblebee

New fruit

Dead flower

Getting riper

Red and perfect for picking

Grow your own tomatoes.

New green fruit

As the tomatoes swell up and become ripe, they change from green to red.

Some tomato plants have fruits that are yellow, orange, purple, dark green, and even striped.

21

Busy Tomato Farm Workers

On a tomato farm, plants are grown in a giant greenhouse.

Inside it is warm all the time, so tomatoes can be grown even in winter.

The greenhouse can be the size of eight football fields and hold 250,000 plants!

°C °F

50 — 120
40 — 100
30 — 80
20 — 60
10 — 40
0
10 — 20
20 — 0
30 — 20

Temperature inside the greenhouse

Thousands of bumblebees are brought to the greenhouse in small cardboard hives.

Hive

Each hive is home to about 100 bees and their queen.

The bees spend their days gathering nectar and pollen to eat.

Bumblebee

Pollen

As they do this, they spread pollen from flower to flower, pollinating the tomato flowers.

Plants for Peppers

We cook crunchy, delicious peppers in stir-fries, Mexican meals, and lots of savory dishes. But how do these fruits grow?

Pepper plant seedling

Pepper plants

In some areas, it's not warm enough to grow peppers all year-round.

In some places, pepper plants are grown in huge greenhouses, where they are protected from cold weather.

A pepper plant can grow to be 13 feet (4 meters) tall and produce 60 peppers.

Tiny new pepper growing

All peppers are green when they start growing.

A pepper turning red

Then they ripen and change color to orange, red, yellow, purple, and chocolate.

Let's Investigate

Tomato or Pepper—which has the most seeds?

Gather your equipment:
- A notebook and pen
- A tomato
- A pepper
- A knife and cutting board
- 2 small plates
- Tweezers

1. Very carefully cut the pepper and tomato in half.

2. Look at the seeds inside each fruit.

Which fruit do you think has the most seeds? Write down your prediction.

How many seeds do you estimate is inside each fruit? Write down your answers.

3. Using your fingers or the tweezers, find the seeds in the tomato and place them on a plate.

4. Repeat with the pepper.

5. Count both sets of seeds.

What are your results? Did they match your prediction or your estimated answers?

Do you think every seed in a tomato or pepper will grow into a new plant? Why or why not?

Why do you think a tomato or pepper plant produces so many seeds?

25

How to Grow Apples

An apple contains seeds that can grow into new apple trees.

However, every apple seed is **unique** and may not grow into the same kind of apple as the fruit it came from.

Seed

For example, the seeds from these gala apples might not produce gala apple trees.

Gala apple

Seeds

This is a problem for farmers because they need to know what kind of apple they are growing.

Gala twig

Tape

Rootstock

To solve this problem, a farmer plants a small young tree called a rootstock.

Then the farmer cuts a twig from a gala tree and slots it into the rootstock.

Gala trees

The twig joins to the rootstock and grows into a new gala tree.

A farm where apples are grown is called an orchard.

Let's Talk

How many different kinds of apples do you think are grown worldwide?

(The answer is on page 32.)

Scrumptious Strawberries

Farmers and gardeners plant strawberry seedlings in soil.

A strawberry farm

The strawberry plants grow lots of leaves and produce white flowers.

New strawberry growing

A tiny strawberry grows from each flower.

Flower

The strawberry grows bigger and bigger. Then it ripens and turns red.

New strawberry

Unripe

Ripe

Runner

Strawberry plants grow shoots called runners that have small leaves and roots.

New plant

The roots grow down into the soil, and each runner becomes a new plant.

Strawberries are fruits with seeds on the outside. Each tiny, yellow, crunchy bit on the outside of a strawberry contains a seed.

Seeds

Packed with Power!

Vegetables and fruits contain **vitamins**, **minerals**, and other good stuff that our bodies need.

These plant foods give us energy and help our bodies fight off illnesses.

Vegetables and fruit contain fiber, which helps you feel full for longer. Fiber also helps your poop move through your intestines.

Green vegetables contain minerals that are good for your blood and keep your bones and teeth strong.

Strawberries and tomatoes keep our hearts healthy.

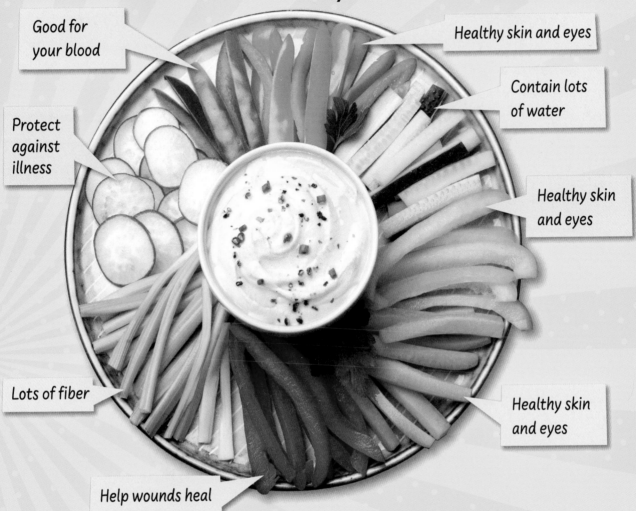

Good for your blood

Healthy skin and eyes

Contain lots of water

Protect against illness

Healthy skin and eyes

Lots of fiber

Healthy skin and eyes

Help wounds heal

Eating a mixture of veggies and fruits every day is a great idea because they all do different jobs!

Let's Test It!

How many different fruits and vegetables can you eat in one week?

Draw a chart and then record every plant food you eat.

	Mon	Tues	Wed	Thur	Fri	Sat	Sun
Breakfast							
Lunch							
Snacks							
Dinner							

Glossary

bud
A small growth on a plant that can grow into a new shoot, leaf, or flower.

bulb
The rounded underground part that some plants grow from. Food for the new plant is stored in the bulb.

community garden
A piece of land gardened by people living near one another that is divided into individual or shared sections for growing vegetables and other plants.

mineral
A kind of nutrient in food, such as iron and calcium, that's important for the body's health and growth.

pollen
A coloured dust that is made by flowers and cones, and is needed for making seeds.

pollinate
To transfer pollen from one flower to another.

roots
Underground parts of a plant that take in water and nutrients from the soil.

seed
A tiny part of a plant that can grow into a new plant.

stem
The main body or stalk of a plant.

unique
One of a kind.

vitamin
A kind of nutrient in food, such as vitamin C or vitamin A, that's important for the body's health and growth.

Index

Answers

Page 19:
Pumpkins, watermelons, cucumbers, and blueberries are all fruits because they have seeds inside. So are avocados and plums, but these fruits just have one large, hard seed. Green beans are actually fruits, too, because there are little seeds, or beans, growing inside them. Parsnips are root vegetables. Leeks are vegetables that are related to onions. A pea pod is a fruit because it's the part of a plant where the seeds grow. However, when we cook and eat pea pods and peas, we think of them as vegetables.

Page 27:
There are 7,500 different kinds of apples grown worldwide.